Back of Bourry

Mark Dobson

DOUBLEDAY
SYDNEY•AUCKLAND•TORONTO•NEW YORK•LONDON

BACK OFF BULLY
A DOUBLEDAY BOOK

First published in May 2002 by Innate Youth.
This edition published by Doubleday in 2003.

National Library of Australia
Cataloguing-in-Publication Entry

Dobson, Mark.
Back off bully.

ISBN 1 86471 085 3.

1. Bullying. 2. Bullying - Prevention. I. Title.

371.58

Transworld Publishers,
a division of Random House Australia Pty Ltd
20 Alfred Street, Milsons Point, NSW 2061
http://www.randomhouse.com.au

Random House New Zealand Limited
18 Poland Road, Glenfield, Auckland

Transworld Publishers,
a division of The Random House Group Ltd
61-63 Uxbridge Road, Ealing, London W5 5SA

Random House Inc
1540 Broadway, New York, New York 10036

Cover design by Darian Causby/Highway 51
Text design and typesetting by Anna Warren, Warren Ventures Pty Ltd
Printed and bound by Ligare Pty Ltd

10 9 8 7 6 5 4 3 2 1

The Author

His name is Mark Dobson
— but everyone calls him Dobbo.

Mark began his career when he was fourteen in a local youth club, which led to several awards and speaking appointments. Since then, he has worked and taught in many countries, including four years at *The Interlocken International Centre for Experiential Education (USA)*. His most recent adventure was with a small team establishing a new university in New York City for gifted teenagers.

Mark has also worked in the remote Aboriginal community of Port Keats in Australia's Northern Territory and led America's largest ever internal cultural exchange program, taking forty inner-city African American students onto a Navajo Indian Reservation for a three-week program.

When he returned to Australia, Mark was invited to attend the prestigious Johnson and Johnson National Youth Leadership Forum in Canberra before he established Innate Solutions, a company which works in schools instilling self-belief in young people, as well as educating large corporations on youth culture. He is also the author of *Rise Above – Tips and Strategies for Teenage Life, Always Forward – Setting Goals and Catching Dreams* and *How to Play Kiss Chasey and Win* (3 Audio CD set) and has worked as a personal coach to Australia's elite Australian Rules footballers.

If you are interested in having Mark speak at your
conference, school or function, call Innate Youth on
(03) 9764 8608 or via dobbo.com.au

Dedication

This book is dedicated to my wonderful friends.

To late-night billycart runs, archery adventures, miniac, Easter egg hunts, seal-launching, the St Joe's program, the pox, tickle fights, darts, late-night pancakes, the Manor and all the fun times that don't have names.

I love you guys. Thank you for making my life so much fun.

Acknowledgements

Thanks to everyone who helped make this book happen. Especially my proofreaders who endure the burden of my complete disregard for spelling and grammar, Ami Bateman, Joanne Dobson (my awesome sister) and Ebony Johnston.

Also to Mick Dunn who was there when I started this project and listened to my excuses for it not being finished.

Thank you crew.

Table of Contents

1 │ Adults Get Bullied

I guess I should start by saying that I know it can be a bit embarrassing to be reading a book on bullying, whether you're a child or an adult. It's not the sort of thing you'll be excited to tell your friends about. To be honest, I never thought I would be writing a book on this subject. It was never my ambition to be an expert on bullying; I wanted to be a fireman just like every other kid my age. However, here I am now, writing a book I didn't plan to write and you are reading a book you never wanted to read. Who would have thought?

Likewise you may be trying to work out who this book is for. Kids? Parents? Business people? Losers? Cry babies? Normal everyday people? This book is for anyone who wants to get treated better by the people around them. It's written for normal everyday people. Just read it and see what happens. If the book is worth it, you'll know.

It may surprise you to know that everyone gets bullied. Everyone. Including parents, business people and sports stars as well as kids at school. As we get older though, we can choose where we hang out and with whom, because we don't have to go to school. At school you have no choice; you have to hang out with bullies whether you like it or not. For this reason, not everyone learns how to stop bullies, they just learn how to get away from them. They think they are over the whole 'bully thing' but they aren't.

Victims of bullying, both kids and adults, often express a feeling of shame or embarrassment for needing advice. The truth is: what would take more courage at school or work, to punch someone or to stand in front of the class and tell them you are reading a book on bullying? Punching, in a weird way, is accepted so it takes no courage, whereas standing in front of the class and talking about an uncool topic is unacceptable and the teasing can be much worse. Same in the workplace. Reading to come to terms with a problem doesn't make you weak, it puts you amongst the smallest part of the population – those who actually do something to take control of their lives.

As for how this book works: I don't want to waste your time so here is a guide to getting the information you need quickly. *Back off Bully* is written for all age groups which means I have tried to use simple language where possible but included very smart and effective strategies. If you want, you can flick through the book and grab bits that interest you or read the whole thing through from start to finish. It's up to you.

To adults in the workplace, let me mention that the strategies in here have had tremendous success so you have picked up the right book. I will refer to situations you may have seen at work but mostly I will use school examples. This is because every age can relate to school bullying but teenagers can't relate to workplace politics. The strategies are fundamental though, regardless of age or environment.

Let the adventure begin.

2 | So What is Bullying ... Really?

> **Many people get bullied but they don't even realise that it's happening.**

Most people seem to think that being bullied means someone is always beating you up or stealing your lunch. That's the sort of bullying you can see but it is more than just someone punching you. It is when people:

Make you do something you don't want to do.

Make you feel a way you don't want to feel.

Treat you in a way that you don't want to be treated.

For example, a bully might make you steal things or make you be mean to other people. Or they might always tell you that it is your fault; that there is something wrong with you; they make fun of you, no matter what you do; nothing is ever good enough.

The most common sort of bullying is when the bully doesn't treat you the way you deserve to be treated. They don't welcome you in games, to after-work drinks, they spread rumours, call you names, hit you or steal your things. Sometimes they copy you, other times they walk away from you or they get people to gang up on you. The common thing is that they always make you feel that what you think, what you do and who you are is not good enough. They make us feel horrible.

It doesn't have to be like this. There are many ways to stop a bully, so we should get started. Let me tell you about a kid I met who was getting badly bullied.

Seriously getting bullied

The first time I really had to help someone who was being bullied was during a work trip. It was about ten in the morning, I was sound asleep after getting to bed late when I heard banging on the door. I was staying at a friend's house in Sydney so I didn't think the visitor would be for me; I just rolled over. The banging continued. I waited a little longer but then the banging turned into banging and crying, so I stumbled out of bed and, looking less than a million dollars, opened the door.

It was a lady from across the street. She had heard I was in town and needed help with her son who was in Year 7. She was crying and apologising for waking me up but she was pretty determined to get my time so I welcomed her in and put the kettle on. It was quite strange: there I was in someone else's house, with one of their neighbours, in my PJs, hair standing on end, offering her a cup of tea and I didn't even know where the teabags were! A typical morning.

As silly as the situation was, the issue with her son was quite real. He had been very happy at primary school, very popular and great at sport. But since going to secondary school, things had gone horribly. He was getting teased every day, being pushed around and punched. This isn't something that always happens when you go to a new school; he had just been unlucky. The teachers had told the boys off but it wasn't working and it had now reached the stage where this boy (let's call him Paul for the sake of the story) was found cutting his wrists in the toilets at school. It had gotten so bad that he wanted to die.

Since then he had seen several psychologists and the teachers had spoken to the boys but little had changed. Earlier that week he had tried to kill himself again. Paul's mother was in tears and desperate, all because a few boys had found it fun to be mean.

That afternoon I met with Paul. He was a great kid and we got on really well. I couldn't believe someone so nice was getting treated so badly. We spent some time together and afterwards, for the first time in over a year, Paul was excited about going to school the next day. He was excited because I had given him things he could do; previously he had thought that dying was the best option. He didn't actually want to die, he just didn't know what else to do. As a matter of fact, he even got up early, sang in the shower and played basketball with his sister before he went to school. His mum thought it was too good to be true.

> He had used the strategies and had no problems at all.

After school I spoke to Paul and sure enough, things had gone perfectly. He had used the strategies and had had no problems at all. One day isn't proof, I know that, but I kept in touch with him for the next week while I was in Sydney and he was having fewer and fewer problems. I ask about him every now and then and he is right on top of it all. He has learnt to deal with it himself, which included calling upon help sometimes, but he had learned the skills to manage tough situations.

The first one of those skills is understanding when you are being bullied. Many people get bullied but they don't even realise that it's happening. They think it's normal.

Especially when we are upset, it is hard to explain what someone is *actually doing* to upset us; all we know is that we feel sad and flat. So here is a crash-course in bullying types so you understand what they are doing and can explain it to someone to get help.

Bullying types

Firstly, you could be bullied in one of these locations: home, school/work or in public. Home and school are pretty obvious places, 'in public' may not be. 'In public' could be waiting for a bus, while at the shops, at a sporting club, at the movies, at a relative's house, a park, a fair etc.

Once you identify *where* you are being bullied, you can then work out what they are doing to make you feel sad or angry. I have found four ways that bullies attack people. They either do it:

> Physically (hurting your body)
>
> Mentally (playing tricks on your brain)

Socially (embarrassing you)

or

Sexually (talking about or touching areas that make you feel uncomfortable)

Often we don't even realise they are picking on us, so here is a closer look at some of the things bullies do.

Physical

Hitting you, kicking you, pushing you, pulling your hair, throwing things at you, twisting your arms, pulling chairs away, flicking your ears or anything else that hurts your body. Pins on chairs, putting things in your food, pulling at your clothes.

Mental

Lying, making you change your mind, breaking your self-confidence, blaming you, making you doubt yourself, telling you that you are ugly, dumb, uncoordinated or un-liked. Making fun of the way you look, your family, race, smell, the amount of money you have, the types of clothes you wear etc.

Social

Making fun of you in front of others, excluding you from groups, embarrassing you, not letting you sit where you want to, spreading rumours, not letting you join in games at school or drinks after work, making fun of your friends, teasing you about the words you use or who you like, making faces at you or saying your name in a dumb voice, teasing you when you stand in front of a group at work or school.

In marriages or romantic relationships, it can often include one person encouraging other family members to treat you as poorly as they do. They may force you to lie to cover for them; invent stories to make out everything is your fault; stop you from going to the shops, out with friends or anywhere you might talk to someone they don't want you to; make rules about who you can speak to or for how long.

Sexual

Making you look at parts of bodies or pictures you don't want to look at. Touching your body in a way that you don't like or don't feel good about. Being asked or forced to touch other people's bodies in a way that you don't want to. People lifting your skirt, pulling down your pants or touching any area usually covered by underwear. Kissing you if you don't want to. Talking to you about sex and different parts of men's and women's bodies when you don't want to. Telling you the things they want to do to your body or what they think of it. Rubbing themselves against you. Asking you about your body, sex life, boyfriends, girlfriends, sexual experiences.

With sexual bullying, the best guide is that if it doesn't feel right to you, presume you are being bullied. Whether it be a conversation or a physical act, you should start to take action as if you are being bullied or abused straight away.

An even clearer guide is that if you have said something like, 'No, I don't want to' or 'Stop it' and it has continued, you are most likely being bullied, with the very slim chance that the person was joking or was accidentally inappropriate.

If you have said 'no' or objected to their behaviour more than three times and it still continues, you are absolutely being bullied and you need to act straightaway: tell someone what happened and start writing down what happened.

3 Bullying Styles

Now we get into a new area – actual types of bullying that people don't recognise or understand. You see, not all bullies work the same and the strategies aren't transferable. You need to know what you're up against. I have found five bullying styles:

> HOT Bullying
>
> On-sight Bullying
>
> Billycart Bullying
>
> Concrete Bullying
>
> Strategic Bullying

HOT Bullying

This comes from the term 'Heat of the Moment.' This is when someone gets suddenly mad and does something mean but it is a once-off incident. It's a serious thing – maybe a fight, a display of intimidation or some horrible words said – but it is over fairly quickly. It's the kind of thing that you need a strategy for in the moment but not long-term.

On-sight Bullying

On-sight bullying is when someone bullies you whenever they see you. They don't seek you out, they just bully everyone around them so when you bump into them you become a possible target. It might be every time you bump into them at a bus stop or in a certain class or when you go to a certain part of the workplace. It's the kind of bullying that you know is going to happen the moment you see the person.

Billycart Bullying

This type of bullying is when the teasing goes on for weeks or months. I call it billycart bullying because it is the kind of bullying that, like a billycart, someone starts pushing but it stops when people get tired of it. It's very real and very common among girls. It is very intense at the start, but fades until it stops completely and then everyone is friends again, pretending the situation never happened.

Concrete Bullying

Concrete bullying is when it is permanently set into your life and is a daily occurrence. It is long-term and there is no indication that it is going to stop. It is constant and can involve everything from having things stolen to being punched, having rumours spread about you, emails insulting you, abuse and intimidation. Unlike on-sight bullying, concrete bullying is an everyday thing and often the bully is looking for you. This can be at home, school, work or other places you go regularly.

Strategic Bullying

This type of bullying is very intense. This is when the bully has made very clear decisions to take friends and other supportive people away from you, so you feel like you have no one on your side. Unlike billycart bullying, this bullying keeps going because the bully keeps it going by inventing more lies, gossip or public anger to keep you feeling sad. It's not the same as concrete bullying. Concrete bullying is thoughtless bullying, when the bully directly attacks you with words or actions. Strategic bullying, on the other hand, is very manipulative. The bully works out what is important to you and gets to those situations or people first. It's vicious. They give you no break from the bullying, involving as much of your life as they can. They really focus on trying to destroy you.

Understanding these categories can help to explain to other people and ourselves what is going on. For example, you can ask:

Where is it happening?

• HOME   • SCHOOL/WORK   • IN PUBLIC

What are they doing?

• PHYSICAL   • MENTAL   • SOCIAL   • SEXUAL

What bullying style?

• HOT   • ON-SIGHT   • BILLYCART

• CONCRETE   • STRATEGIC

So now at least you can explain to teachers, your boss, friends or family exactly what is going on. Most important of all, it may now be clear to you.

You want some juicy stuff now? Well, the best place to start is by telling you the things that bullies *don't* want you to know. I call them 'The Three Bully Secrets'. The first one is ...

4 | The First Bully Secret

Just about every time I work with someone who is being bullied and ask them what they want help with, the common answer is: to show them how to beat up the bully or get back at them. Often, adults are just happy for it to stop but kids especially want revenge.

I understand this but I laugh because it's not going to happen. If you did this, it would make you no better than the bully. It means that if you were able to, you would bully them. But you don't want to become the bully. You want to stop them so you can get on with your life.

It's important to understand that you can't beat a bully at being a bully. The bully was a bully before you and they are really good at it. You can try all you like but it is unlikely that you will ever beat them because violence and manipulative games are their specialty. The good guys beat up bullies in the

17

movies but real life isn't always quite the same; the good guys win but not through violence. Just like you wouldn't be able to beat an Olympic runner or swimmer – they are really good at their events and even if you trained really hard, they have a mental edge over you.

You beat a bully by stopping them. Let me explain.

Adults are happy for bullying to stop but kids want revenge.

We want to take revenge on a bully because they have made us angry by being mean. I explain it by saying they give us 'meanness'. Like Santa gives away presents and fairies give away magic dust, bullies give out 'meanness'. They have to give it out because it causes them pain to keep it. They don't want it so they give it away.

When a bully is mean to you, it can build up inside yourself and if you don't release your anger it becomes 'rage'. Rage is the emotion that makes us want to get the bully back, but the problem is, rage is hard to control. We are so worked up that if we try to let it out, it just floods us with tears, yelling and wild punches, shaking and then snot comes out of our nose and we look like a fool.

So the two reasons why you won't beat the bully at being a bully is because:

> 1. They are the bully, not you, so they have more meanness to give.

> 2. By the time you are serious about doing something about the situation it's no longer anger, which is manageable, it is rage, which is uncontrollable ... and comes with snot.

Bullies also feel rage but not towards you. They feel it towards the person who has been mean to them or because of horrible things that have happened to them. They feel rage toward the situation or person that made them a bully in the first place. Maybe a mean parent, brother, sister, or even anger at themselves. The problem is, they are so angry at their enemy that they can't express it without losing control, so they release their anger on you. You are not the cause of their rage so they can stay calm when they are mean, even though you might get really worked up at them; they feel angry but in control.

Being mean to you is their way of getting rid of the rage that's inside them. The meanness is not aimed at you because you are ugly or un-co or incompetent, it's because they want to give it to anyone who won't give it straight back. When they give it to you they feel powerful.

So, back to where I started. You can't beat a bully at being a bully because to do that you would need more meanness inside you than they have. They are the ones giving you the meanness and like a bank giving out money, they will always have more money than you. To overcome them, you have to stop wanting to beat them at their own game. You just want them to stop so you can get on with your life. To do that you need to know The Second Bully Secret. This one is really important.

5 The Second Bully Secret

Bullies pull hair, spread rumours and make you stay late at work because they want a reaction. It's not the only reason but it's the biggest one. They may not realise it, but there is nothing satisfying about giving away meanness without a response.

When you give a present to someone at Christmas, the best response is a huge smile and lots of enthusiasm about how great the gift is. It's the *reaction* that makes it fun – or not fun – to give. The same at a family function: when you throw a water bomb, you throw it at the person who will give the best reaction and/or who you want a reaction from. In a water fight, there is no point in throwing a water bomb at someone who is already wet. You always look for someone who doesn't want to get wet because they will give the funniest reaction.

Bullies are the same. They love seeing you get worked up or change your behaviour due to them, whether it be forcing you

21

to re-write a report for your boss, falling over in the playground or bursting into tears. Bullies love how they can do something small, and in response you do something over the top like yell or fight or cry or become obviously weak. They love the reaction! So when you don't react, they get annoyed first and then bored.

> **Bullies pull hair and spread rumours because they want a reaction.**

For instance, have you ever been at a BBQ and tried to put sauce on your meal with one of those plastic squeeze bottles? You squeeze and some sauce comes out – which is the reaction you want – so you squirt again. What if nothing comes out? You give it a shake and squirt again and again until it's blowing more air than sauce, and eventually you realise it's pointless so you get a different bottle.

This is just the same for a bully: they want a reaction from you. When they don't get it they try harder, just like you would with a sauce bottle. Until eventually they find another person to bully or they don't bother any more.

This applied to Paul's situation whom I mentioned earlier. The bullies came and pushed him around expecting a reaction but this time they didn't get one. He had learned this rule and promised himself he wouldn't react. The thing is that these bullies had come to Paul so many times, they were sure that if they squeezed him enough, eventually he would react. So they got meaner with him and tougher but Paul stayed strong until eventually the bullies realised he was no fun. They came back every day or two but there was no longer a reaction so eventually they left Paul alone. I will talk more about the strategy later. For now I just want you to understand the bully: they want a reaction.

Lastly, you need to know The Third Bully Secret.

6 | The Third Bully Secret

Bullies feel tall by making you feel small.

Imagine if a bully had to carry all their meanness in a sack on their back instead of inside of them. A heavy sack would make it difficult for them to stand up straight so they would have to walk on their knees instead. Compared to everyone else, the bully would feel short. By short, we don't mean their height. 'Short' is how good someone feels about themselves.

When anyone has to carry a bag of meanness they feel bad and doubt that they are a good person. They ask themselves, 'If I was a good person, why would people be mean to me? I have been given so much meanness that I must be a bad person.'

When people are mean to you, it's not because you are a bad person. It's because they are so sad, they need to give their meanness away to anyone who won't give it back. They think that by giving away meanness and by making others feel sad, they won't feel as bad as they do.

They are wrong. Making others feel unhappy only makes you feel worse. At first they think it feels good but later, when they are alone, they start to realise how bad it feels. They never admit it, usually because they don't realise the link between their mean actions and sadness. But they are absolutely linked. Just think about when you do something nice for someone; you feel good for the rest of the day, even when you're on your own. Well, the same is true for when we do something bad: we feel bad for the rest of the day. Bullies feel bad a lot.

> When people are mean to you it's because they are sad and need to give their meanness away.

Bullies hate feeling short so instead of giving the meanness back to the person who gave it to them and standing up like everyone else, the bully has another plan. The bully decides that instead of trying to be tall, they will make everyone else short just like them. That way, they will never feel small because everyone would be the same. Therefore they share their meanness so that everyone is carrying heavy sacks and everyone is short – and sad.

In real terms, this means that a bully will be mean to you if you do anything they don't like; for example, talking to someone they don't like, wearing something they would be too scared to wear or working differently to them. The bully will then throw meanness at you so that you don't outshine them or make them feel small. If you try to be more than them, they will give you more meanness to weigh you down.

So I've just given you a basic understanding of what goes on in a bully's head. The next things we need to know are the tricks they use to be mean. If you are like most people, often someone can make you feel sad but you have no idea how they are doing it. You sort-of know but when you tell a teacher, explain it to a parent or talk to the bully about it, it never sounds like a big deal. They bully you in such a clever way that you look weak if you say anything because what they are doing is almost invisible. They bully you in a way that you can't prove.

Well, you'll be able to prove it now because this next section shows you exactly how they do it. There are three tricks that just about every bully uses and here they are.

7 | The Tricks Bullies Use

Bullies are people who intentionally cause pain.

Once you know how a magic trick works, the fun is taken out of the trick. The magician also gets mad when you reveal the magic because the trick doesn't work anymore.

The bully is just the same. If you know the tricks, it takes the pain away and the bully isn't as effective. Their words don't hurt anywhere near the same when you know they are using a standard bullying strategy. They are not even being clever. Here are three of the most common tricks that bullies use.

The disclaimer

This is your basic trick. Anyone can do it and just about every bully does. This is when the bully pretends that they aren't doing anything wrong or that it is all either your fault or in your head. They say things like:

Can't you take a joke?

Don't be such a cry-baby!

We were just messing around.

You started it first.

I don't know what you're talking about.

As if!

You do it more than I do. You're always mean!

(Sarcastic) Yeah! Like I'm soooo mean to you.

You're an idiot!

Well, you're annoying us.

At work, it's a little more 'adult' in language but it's the same thing. They often blame upper management, another department or something you did previously for their present behaviour. They especially love to keep referring to the one mistake you made ages ago, never letting you forget it.

I wouldn't have to bring it up if it was done right the first time.

And you're perfect, are you?

Sorry ... didn't you get my email about after-work drinks? I am sure I sent it.

If you didn't take such long tea breaks you would know what's going on.

If you can't handle the pressure maybe you should be working somewhere else.

You tell me you want to be treated better, but you can't even handle a little bit of criticism.

And I suppose all the mistakes in that report are my fault too.

You say you want opportunity, but as soon as it gets tough you can't handle it.

This is the real world, honey.

I wasn't informed.

If everyone met budget with me being nice, I would be.

Do you think I like having to check up on you all the time?

At home it's different again. Parents use excuses that their children can't understand or argue against, such as telling their child that the kid's personality or appearance is the problem.

I wouldn't have to get mad if you weren't so horrible.

I work all day for you and I just want to rest. Do you want me to work more? Is that what you want?

If your mother didn't spend every cent I earn, I wouldn't be so stressed!

And you, young lady! If it wasn't for your complaining maybe your dad would still be here!

If you weren't so naughty I wouldn't have to hit you so hard.

You ruined my life when you were born.

I hate looking at you!

If you weren't so ugly I wouldn't need to be so mean!

Do you know how embarrassing it is being seen with you?

This technique is very common. It's such a simple way to make wrong behaviour seem like nothing at all while making the whole situation your fault.

You'll find that most of the things bullies do can't be proved, which is why this simple strategy works for them. For instance, they might turn their back on you when you want to join a group or they might walk away with their friends to tell secrets or not kick the ball to you. When you bring up their behaviour, they can pretend that you're dreaming it up because you can't prove it. If they were excluding you, and you mentioned it, they might say something like:

'WHEN? When did I ever?'

If we reply with:

'Before, when you walked away with Kate!'

They are likely to pretend they didn't by saying something like:

'We were just walking! Aren't you even allowed to walk anymore?! You're so selfish. Hey Kate, were we telling secrets before? No! See. Why don't you stop being such a sticky-beak and let people just talk?'

In this situation, the bully has pretended they didn't do it and turned the situation back on you. She also got her friend involved, which I call the **round-up** technique (we'll talk about that next). So the final outcome is that you look mean for bringing it up and they can continue to bully because if you bring it up again you look mean again.

Boys tend to respond a little differently. Among immature guys, sharing pain or problems is considered a weakness. I know it shouldn't be like this but guys don't often learn to share feelings like girls do, and those who express themselves are often attacked. If you point out to a male bully that he is always flicking your ears, forcing you to stay at work late or is generally intimidating, he will assume an even stronger role, and respond by either saying something like, 'So what?' or 'No I don't!' and then doing it again straightaway. Because you reacted and asked him to stop, he now has even more reason to do it because he has seen weakness and male bullies will always target weakness.

Whether it's targeting boys or girls the bullying strategy is the same: it's about pretending that nothing is going on, and if there's anyone to blame, it's you.

The round-up

The next one is the round-up. It's when the bully runs off and rounds up as many people as possible to be on their side, thinking that the more allies they have, the greater their chance of winning and the more popular they will be.

When a bully can't get rid of their bag of meanness they try to get a bigger bag of people liking them. They feel better if they think that everyone hates someone else; it means less people hate them. So they organise someone to hate.

The way the round-up usually works is after a phonecall or a conversation with you, they use what you said against you. (Or sometimes they just invent information.) They contact everyone and spread a rumour to get them onside and make you out to be incredibly mean. They might say something like:

> 'Monica is so mean, she is always telling lies. She's not our friend anymore is she? I only pretended to like her to be nice. You don't like her, do you?'

The next day you come to school or work and are greeted by a weird silence; no one is talking to you.

It isn't always after a conversation, it can also happen when your friends spend time together and you are not there. They can forget how great you are and be negative about you. This is when you might have to hang out with your 'part-time friends' because all your usual friends have ganged up on you.

With guys it's a little different. Girls tend to take a side when the round-up happens and participate in the emotion or gossip that's taking place. Guys, on the other hand, go silent. It's more a case of following a leader. The bully becomes the leader and excludes some unfortunate person from footy, from lunch or from a meeting. He then calls the other guys to follow him, saying something like:

> 'Come on guys, let's leave this loser' or ...

> 'Let's play footy. Not you idiot, you're a loser.'

Both comments have a statement which points out a 'direction' or an 'action' everyone should take. And there is often a direction statement for the person being bullied; it's usually something like:

> 'You're not hanging around with us! Go away!' or
>
> 'Go sit down, idiot!'

The bully decides what the group is going to do and then people do it; he becomes their leader.

In the workplace it's more like:

> 'Smoko guys.' Then he turns to one person. 'What do you think you're doing? You're a slacker, get back to work! You have to earn smoko.'

It is worth mentioning at this point that it's easy not to realise that the behaviour I've just described is bullying, especially if it's never happened to you. That's how clever the trick is. You'd probably just assume that the tension exists only between those two people. It never clicks that the leader is getting a bunch of people together to gang up on someone else. Nor did you think you were supporting a bully when you went to smoko, played footy or listened to the rumours. Bullies aren't always mean-looking people who wear black and punch people. Bullies are people who intentionally cause pain. The clever bullies make it look like they are the ones being bullied. Tricky buggers, bullies.

'Poor me' or 'The guilt-trip'

This one is just as simple as the others; however, it traps many more people. The bully mainly uses it to defend themselves when they are getting in trouble for being a bully or when you are trying to point out that they are wrong. This strategy involves making us feel sorry for them, or guilty, instead of angry. If you have managed to point out they are wrong and they have no way of defending themselves, they may start saying things like this as they burst into tears:

> 'You don't understand! My whole life is horrible! Mum hates me. Dad hates me. I'm never going to get all my homework done and that cow over there has told everyone that I hate her and now you hate me too!'

At a workplace, it's done very cleverly. It's hard to detect but a typical example is when they need you to stay back but they don't want to pay you or you have challenged their management and they bring out the sob story about meeting budgets and working long hours.

Essentially, in this strategy they are bringing in emotion to defend themselves and it plays on our kind nature. Here is another classic example:

> 'I didn't mean to be rude, it's just that it's the anniversary of my mother's death next week and this time of year makes me upset. I just have so much on and the kids are struggling at school …'

Looks like a genuine excuse, doesn't it? It's the oldest trick in the book, bringing in the sick or deceased loved one. It's their trump card, you see, because you can't argue with it without seeming insensitive. I even look insensitive for bringing it up.

In my presentations and workshops, endless numbers of people admit they have been guilty of doing this. Some other creative excuses include doctor's appointments, a sick spouse, personal illness, migraines, coffee withdrawal, chronic fatigue or anything else that can't be proved and is sensitive to talk about. One guy swallowed a coin when he was a kid and anytime he needed to, he claimed the coin was lodged in a more painful part of his stomach. Ridiculous.

I am not saying these people are lying, but they are stretching the impact of these obstacles to include behaviours they should simply take responsibility for. Instead, they take a sensitive situation which can't be proved and wave it around like a badge of permission.

By doing this, they try to make us think that their treatment of us is okay because things are so bad in their lives. They make you feel guilty for making them feel worse.

By using this strategy, bullies can get away with shirking their responsibilities. We back off and say things like:

'It's not their fault, it's because of ...'

or we see their tears and say things like:

'I think they are sorry for what they have done.
Let's just forget about it.'

Don't get me wrong. I am not against giving sympathy but my point is, this is a bullying strategy that gets bullies out of trouble and makes you feel guilty or that it is okay to be treated badly. This point is especially relevant to sexual bullying. It is very common for the bully to make their victim feel like it is their fault or that the bullies are entitled to do horrible things so that they can cope with life. It is never true. There is never a reason for someone to get bullied, especially sexually. NEVER. In this situation, use the journal strategy, which I will tell you about shortly.

To summarise the guilt-trip strategy: the bully blows everything out of proportion. They dream up problems and go on about how hard their life is. They essentially tell you a story of why they did what they did. It's a *story* though. There is some truth in it but rarely is it a legitimate excuse. However, it is a very good distraction from the issue and a way for them to avoid admitting that they are wrong. They may feel a great deal of pressure or sadness but this is not an excuse for bad behaviour, especially if the problem has nothing to do with you.

Okay, now it is time for the good stuff. Strategies to stop a bully in their tracks.

8 | Strategy 1

It's about how you stand.

Have you ever had someone tell you to stand up straight or sit up smart? This is because our brain and body are linked and although we don't realise it, how we feel is shown through our bodies. Therefore, we can tell people are sad just by looking at them and reckon some people are tough even though they haven't said anything. Here is what I mean.

When I was working with Paul, I told him to imagine he was getting bullied. We imagined the bullies had circled him and were pushing him, that they were calling him names and he was starting to cry. Paul was almost in tears and just as he started to cry, I told him to open his eyes and look at his reflection in the window. He saw himself, head down deep, arms folded across his stomach, weight on one foot, shoulders down and scrunched together. We took note of all the features and then we did another visualisation.

This time we remembered a time when he had kicked a goal in his winning grand final and he was receiving his medal. This time when I got him to look at his reflection it was quite different. He was six centimetres taller, his head was high and his shoulders were back. Both feet were holding his weight and were firmly planted on the ground. His hands were held together in front of him and there was no way this kid was moving for anyone.

So for some time we practised this new way of standing. I teased him and got really nasty and he kept standing the new way. I pushed him and shook him and I became nastier and nastier so that he got used to the new stance in pressure situations. The more we did it the stronger and stronger he got. It was really exciting. We practised the stance walking and sitting down and playing sport until he knew what to do with his body in all situations. It was the first time he had been trained to defend himself against bullying.

If you remember Paul's story, he was getting bullied a great deal. So you might find it hard to believe that this strategy would stop the bullies from hitting him. You're right. They still came after him but this time Paul stood strong and didn't react like he used to. He acted as if they bored him and stood tall as they teased until eventually they got sick of him and left. He also used the other strategies I am about to explain but this one is first and is vital.

In the workplace, the same strategy applies. When you are called into the boss's office, there is great power in walking in at your own pace. Tall, shoulders back, eyes up, but calm and certain at the same time. If you are not sure how to sit or stand at a time when you need to be respected, think of someone you know who would handle the situation well and pretend you are them. How would they sit? What mannerisms would they use?

> Think of a time you felt strong and confident and pretend you are in that moment again.

In the workplace especially, this strategy needs to be used every day. If you stand up tall for yourself once but walk like a pushover most of the time, you become less believable.

Using this strategy at home is effective but needs to be thought through carefully. If you stand up to your parents you may receive a swift hit or possibly make them madder. Parents always expect to be the authority and they will fight viciously to remain in control, especially if you are still a student. The way to use a confident stance at home is to use it only when your parents are wrong, and not when you just don't like what they say.

For example, if they are giving you an instruction about the smooth running of the house, such as:

> It's time to brush your teeth.
>
> Clean up that mess you made, please.
>
> Please put shoes on your little sister.

… then you just need to help. These things have to be done and are about needing your help around the house rather than about bullying. When this is the case, standing up tall and saying 'no' may get you in some trouble.

When you believe your parents are wrong, then it's time to stand up tall and proud in a manner that shows you are right. When parents are mean, make you do all the work, touch you in a way that you don't like, hit you or do any of the things we have talked about in the book so far, they are wrong and you need to stand up tall to them.

A good way to do this, despite your age or environment, is to think of a time you felt strong and confident and pretend you are in that moment again. Look in a mirror and notice what you are doing with your body. When you later need to stand tall, you'll know what to do. A great tip is to always stand up to make your point. If your parent, uncle, auntie, carer, grandparent or boss is being mean to you and you are sitting or lying down, get to your feet and stand up. They may not like this, but your stance will make them reconsider their point.

This strategy is just step one and is vital but you really need to use all the strategies together so the next strategy is …

9 | Strategy 2

Remember how bullies love a reaction? Well, if you don't give them one, they get bored.

It's very common for people to feel great power and satisfaction when they leave their mark in some way. Some people love to run into a flock of birds and watch them fly away, some love to bang drums and some love to scratch the side of a car with a key. Each experience has us feeling that we left an impact. If the birds didn't fly away, the drums didn't make noise and the car didn't scratch, no one would bother doing it.

The same when the bully annoys you: if there is no reaction, it's no fun.

Let's take a bunch of girls who have started picking on a particular girl. They pull her hair from behind her, they lie to get her into trouble, they write notes and spread rumours. The same rule applies: don't react. Don't yell and scream, don't burst into tears, don't spread rumours about them and don't fight back. Don't react. Just act as if it is all childish and go with the flow.

When I suggest this strategy at schools and workplaces, people always challenge me, saying things like, 'So if someone tells everyone that I am a slut, am I just meant to do nothing? That's stupid!'

It's not stupid at all. Think about it.

If a huge battleship sails into port and is being fired at by a man on the shore's edge, do you think the ship captain will care about the bullets bouncing off the hull? He won't like being shot at but the gun is powerless against a battleship so he can just ignore the gunman.

What if that same captain was rowing an inflatable raft past the same man with the gun? That captain is going to call 'battle stations' because he recognises that he is weak and needs to defend himself. You see: the weak defend, the strong ignore and if the strong do have to act, they do it calmly and with very little effort. When you get worked up, you admit weakness and the bully will keep shooting. When you don't react you are saying, 'I am strong and above your petty behaviour.'

I realise there is more to it than this and that bullies have other strategies to combat being ignored but this is a start and is powerful when used with the other tools.

'But you have to do something!' I hear you say. Yes – either act bored, or as if their behaviour is simply stupid. For example, imagine that an Important Person was about to make a speech live on TV and they are running late. They are sprinting down the corridor to get to the studio when someone stops them and says:

> 'Excuse me, everyone says the sky is blue but
> I think it's red, what do you think?'

This Very Important Person is going to be dumbfounded that someone could waste their time with such a question. They wouldn't get mean or angry, they would just look at them in disbelief and then hurry on their way. They probably wouldn't even bother to speak, they would just shake their head and keep going. This is how you must respond, too.

What if the bullies won't leave you alone? What if you act as if their behaviour is stupid but they follow you or keep doing it? Well, what do you think the Very Important Person would do if the silly person kept annoying them? Let's see. Say they continue to run to the studio and are stopped again.

> 'Well, what do you think? Is the sky red or blue?'

Their reaction would be the same; they would be thinking 'this is ridiculous' and say something like:

> 'I haven't got time for this', 'I'm in a hurry'

or maybe

> 'I'm busy now, I'll talk later.'

Either way, they still don't react to the question or answer it. They act, but they don't *re-act* by responding the way the bully expects. The Important Person sees the question as trivial and quite stupid. This is how we must react to the constant bully.

What if they keep doing it even more?

Well, what if our Important Person was going to miss the timeslot for his speech? What would they do? First, I expect they would be stern and say something like:

> 'This situation is ridiculous. Play your silly games somewhere else and waste your own time. I have things to do.'

And if the silly person continued, the Important Person would call 'security', which is the same as calling to a teacher, parent, friend or boss. When you request help don't 'dob' and cry, instead tell them that the bully is being silly. Say something like:

> 'Miss, I have spoken to Jason but he just keeps being silly and pestering me. I am not mad but he is being ridiculous. Could you please say something to him before it gets serious?'

Likewise at work:

> 'I have asked Sarah Jackson to stop with her unreasonable requests but she continues. It's quite exhausting and ridiculous and we need to get this sorted out before it becomes a bigger issue, involves other people and costs the company money.'

See, when I say 'don't react' you can still act as long as you don't do anything that the bully wants you to do, and don't let their actions affect your life. Sometimes this can be tough but it does get easier. When we say something to the bully, teacher or boss, it needs to be calm and controlled. Managed anger is fine, as long as you come across calm and clear-thinking. The bullying may very well affect your mood but we must never let the bully know. Maybe later but never at the time. Not getting angry in the moment takes practice but if you always treat bullies like this and never react, you will also find that you don't get as mad because it doesn't build up. It actually gets easier.

So in summary: don't burst into tears, yell, scream, hit back or carry on; it will never help. Always be very calm and seemingly bored by their behaviour. If the bullying continues, respond as little as possible and make it clear you think their behaviour is stupid. If this doesn't do the job, call security.

10 | Strategy 3

Don't Argue, Just Agree

Have you ever arrived at school or work to find a rumour has been spread about you? It can even be a stupid one like, 'OOOOooooo, you love Simon.' The next thing you know, you are arguing that you *don't* love Simon – which you know to be true but you have been tricked into an argument. You may not even know who Simon is but you still have to claim that you don't love him because otherwise everyone will think it is true. This means that someone can make up anything and you have to take the other side. It's crazy! They say, 'You're dumb', you argue you're smart. They say, 'You have blue hair', you argue you don't. They argue, 'You eat crayons', you argue you don't. You end up fighting to prove something that is obvious. People can tell you don't have blue hair!

So the strategy is: don't argue, just agree. An argument has two sides – theirs and yours. If you don't take a side, it is no longer an argument, it's just an opinion and the bully will get bored because you aren't reacting.

Let's take a tougher example. Even though this is a schoolyard example, it's the same for adults, just a different setting and more sophisticated language. We'll do an adult example in a moment.

A friend of mine, Liz, arrived at school to find the entire year level hating her. A new girl at school, Sarah, had tried to fit in by telling everyone that Liz had kissed three guys on the weekend. Sarah also claimed that even though Liz knew her best friends liked the boys, she kissed them anyway. She told Liz's best friends that Liz had been gossiping about them and telling the guys all of their secrets.

As you can imagine, this was one serious situation for Liz. It may sound silly and childish, but when it's your world, it feels very painful when your friends don't trust you. When Liz arrived at school (an all girls' school) not a single person was speaking to her. She was thrown horrible looks in the corridor, people stopped speaking when she entered a room and desks were covered in graffiti about her. The girls then went to all the guys they knew and made up stories about Liz so that they ended up hating her too. This went on for almost three months.

This is a classic case of strategic bullying because the bully went to anyone Liz knew and lied to them first.

Liz only contacted me after it had been going on for three months. Before then, she was too embarrassed to ask for help because she felt like a loser with no friends and too many problems. She was never a loser but she did have a big problem on her hands.

I'll tell you how we got out of this one but the first thing I said to Liz was: don't argue and don't defend yourself in an argument. Stand like an important person, as if all of this commotion is trivial but don't take a side. I say this for two reasons:

> 1. The strong and those who are right don't need to defend themselves (remember the battleship example). By not arguing people start to see that.

> 2. For an argument or a fight to exist it needs two sides.

Like I said earlier: whenever we say, 'No, I don't love Simon' or 'I didn't say that!' we start an argument. Until we give our side of the story it is merely someone else's opinion. The moment we give our side, it becomes an argument. An argument is a reaction which is what the bully wants. When we don't argue, we deprive the bully of the opportunity to distort our words and turn them back on us. Instead, we simply agree with their opinion. We don't say that it is *right*, we just let them have their viewpoint.

Imagine, for a moment, that you were Liz. You turned up to school and someone met you in the corridor with a group of their friends and started yelling:

> 'You hate Kim! Sarah told us. Just because you kissed someone doesn't mean they like you! Now everyone hates you!'

To say something like this, the bully would have to be pretty worked up and would only do it if they had a bunch of friends to back them up. What you need to realise here is that they are looking for a reaction. They are yelling and screaming at you, which usually gets a response. The cool thing is that if one person yells and screams, they look stupid but if two people do, it's an argument and as long as both people act the same, anything goes. If both people are crying, it is okay; if only one person is, they are over-reacting. If both people are violent, it is a fight; if one is, it is considered assault. If someone is yelling at you, they want you to yell too so that they don't look stupid. So whatever you do, *don't yell* and *don't argue*. **It's the 'don't react' strategy plus the 'don't argue' strategy**. Instead I suggest you just say:

'What?'

Ask as if you have no idea what they are talking about. This isn't arguing, it isn't yelling, they can't disagree with you; it gives you time to think. The attacker always has more to say because they are so worked up. (Remember, people can't control rage so let them go.)

> 'Sarah told us about you on the weekend. We thought we could trust you but you're just a slut! No one likes you! We spoke to the guys and they hate you too and Steven doesn't want you to go to his party anymore.'

Now you have to respond, but you don't have to argue! Never get worked up, just play it small. There are two ways to do it.

1. Ask questions and always be surprised by the answers.

2. Act as if the whole thing bores you.

Never add anger or 'meanness' to your words. Your enemy is going to presume anything you say is mean anyway and exaggerate your words to others, so don't help them. If you have been mean at all it will only make things worse. Remember, you can't beat a bully at 'meanness'. Even if you have a rough idea about what they are saying, try this:

> 'I'm sorry, I'm not sure what you mean. (Calm – puzzled) What
> did I do?'

> 'You called Kim a bitch and told the boys all of Sally and Fiona's
> secrets! And!!! ... you kissed Theo and you knew that Sarah
> liked him for ages.'

Now act surprised then ask another question.

> 'Oh? Who said I did that?'

By doing this, the bully gets all their anger out and you don't actually commit to anything. I am not suggesting it is going to be easy or that you're out of trouble but at least you won't make things worse and you'll get all the information you need.

Eventually the bully will do one of two things: either ask for a response from you or just storm off, really mad. People love doing this because they think it puts an exclamation mark to their argument. It also lets them run off if they are embarrassed and have nothing left to say. If they do storm off, just let it go. They will continue to gossip about you but leave it for now. I'll show you more on this later.

If they ask for a response, still don't give your side of the story; you don't want an argument. Just repeat what they have said and agree. For example:

'Well, I don't know what to say. Apparently Sarah thinks that I have upset a lot of people.'

'You have.'

'So everyone says.'

'They are not "saying", you did!'

'Well, you have already made your minds up. I can't argue with that.'

It goes on and on. Just don't argue and there can be no conflict. I am not saying *never* argue but unless it is a really *huge* deal, there is just no need. The truth *always* comes out. Always! If you react to their opinion though, you will be arguing all the time.

Every second Wednesday night I used to run a mini-seminar called 'Live More' for teenagers, which deals with this sort of information. On one occasion, we covered arguments and I challenged everyone to be argument-free for 24 hours. The feedback was amazing! People found it really tough, but more interesting was their amazement at how many arguments they were having during the day that they just didn't need.

I am not saying never argue. Just don't be tricked into arguing about things that are ridiculous.

So you can see how effective this is, I want to show you how I used this on the street one day. I had just pulled into a petrol station to get a few things and when I was walking out, I noticed three kids pumping up the tyres on some billycarts they had made. I went over and started chatting to them but after a couple of minutes, I heard a huge engine roar and a screech of brakes. To my right, stopped in the exit lane of the garage, was a hotted-up Torana and its owner slamming his door and storming towards me. He looked mean and he was mad at me about something. I seized up with fear, which really didn't help a whole lot. As he raged at me with his fist raised, I managed to figure out why he was so angry. It appears that I had been standing with my back to the bowsers and when he had tried to drive past, I was blocking his way. He thought I was doing it intentionally.

As he got closer, it became obvious that he was wired on drugs. His eyes were dark and bloodshot and his skin was covered with sores. In very strong language he was telling me what a dumb person I was. Straightaway, the moment before he made to hit me, I agreed.

> 'You're right mate. I don't know what I was thinking. No wonder you're mad! I was completely in your way. I should have been able to see you. I'm really sorry, mate!'

As I said this, he became confused and although he was still mad, his brain didn't know what to do. He wasn't expecting my response. Just as I saw his bewilderment, I slipped in the old …

> 'Great car, must have cost you a fortune. Did you do it all yourself?'

He now had to respond to me instead of me to him, and he didn't know what to say. Mind you, I still wasn't feeling safe.

> 'What?! Just don't do it again!!! Alright?!'

> 'Yeah, I am sorry mate, I was out of line. Won't happen again.'

And it was over. Sure, I had to swallow my pride but much better than swallowing knuckles.

It works every time. Don't argue, just agree and it takes the heat out of the moment.

Key point

You will notice that I never put myself down. I didn't argue with what he said but I never said I was dumb. If one of his friends had said:

> 'Hey. You just said you're dumb.'

I could reply:

58

'I agreed that he couldn't get through, that he could think I was dumb for that, but I never said I'm dumb.'

If they disagree and say:

'That's the same thing.'

Just agree ...

'If you think so.'

Following are some useful responses. They aren't come-back lines; come-back lines are attacking. These extinguish the situation.

- ▶ If you say so.
- ▶ I can't argue with that.
- ▶ That's a pretty strong argument.
- ▶ Who would have thought all of that could happen.
- ▶ I understand how it could look like that.
- ▶ I have nothing to say.
- ▶ That's a pretty good point.
- ▶ I'll have to give that some thought.
- ▶ I'll have to get back to you on that.

▶ What?

▶ I agree.

▶ We disagree and that's okay.

Remember though, tone of voice is very important. Don't be smart or mean, just don't argue.

The strategy can be applied to any situation. For example, let's say there is speculation at work that you are intentionally making someone look incompetent. There is a new computer system which you have learnt easily but someone else is struggling. In their frustration, they begin to suggest that you are arrogant and self-important. You come to work to a strange mood followed by:

'So…what…are you Mr. Computer genius now? You don't have to throw it in our face!'

'I'm sorry, what are we talking about?'

'As if you don't know! You strut around as if you're so smart. People can see through you. Jack's been here for fifteen years, it's going to take more than a couple of lucky key punches to get his job!'

The next words that come out of your mouth are vital. Typically, we come in and defend ourselves with something like, 'Get stuffed. All I did was my job. If he can't keep up that's his problem.' Which is true but it's going to inflame the situation. Instead, go for the 'don't argue' policy until you can take proper action later.

> 'Wow, do people really think I want his job?'

> 'Don't start acting all innocent with me. Your smart-alec smile won't get you out of this one. There are a lot of people around here who have had enough of you. You better watch your back, son. You have crossed the line on this one.'

> 'I don't know what to say, this is all news to me. I am sorry everyone sees it like this. How can we get it sorted out?'

Once again, don't argue. Play it calm. No point infuriating people. You might know the situation is ridiculous but they are ready for a fight and you are outnumbered. A good tactic is to ask for advice, as in that last sentence. It will speed up the resolution.

All right, time for strategy 4.

11 Strategy 4

Not arguing is a start but it still hasn't got us out of trouble. If we go back to the example of Liz, she isn't out of deep water yet. There is more to do. So I needed to find out from Liz if she understood Strategy 4 – don't throw stones. By which I mean: have you been nasty in the past.

People are less likely to throw stones at you if you don't throw stones yourself. For example, if you have a reputation for never being mean to people, but then one day someone starts being nasty to you, how do you think others would respond? Most likely, they would see the bully as mean and you as innocent.

If someone starts spreading malicious rumours about you, people might believe the stories if they have seen you do similar things before. For example, if they tell a teacher that you are making up lies and last week you *were* making up lies, then the teacher will find it hard to believe your innocence. The same if the claim is that you hit them. If you usually do hit people then others will expect it to be true.

These are all pretty obvious examples but the most common mistake is when socialising.

When you are in a group and everyone is gossiping or telling stories, you can learn a lot about your friends. Always remember: the way they talk about other people is how they talk about you when you are not there. If they say nice things about others and stand up for those who aren't around, then they will be doing the same for you. If they are mean about people who aren't there, you can bet they are doing the same to you.

This is a good way to see if you can trust your friends but my main point is this: if you always speak highly of people and are never mean, if you stick up for your friends and always look out for them, then people will find it hard to believe nasty rumours about you. This is what I mean by being untouchable. People can't get you because you are a nice person and everyone knows it. And being a good person isn't hard; all you have to do is speak well of people when they are not there – and mean it. Say and do kind things and be sincere. This is all it takes to be nice. By doing this, you become untouchable because no one will believe the bad things said about you.

As for Liz: she felt that she was untouchable but I knew her and although she was a lovely girl, she could be mean sometimes, too. Her idea of untouchable was different from mine. So here is the next part of the rule: Be an important friend.

Be an important friend

Try to be the most important friend to your friends. Make yourself indispensible so that your friends would never be mean to you. Here's why.

At school, for every nice thing said, there are ten nasty comments. On average; at some schools it is more. Workplaces aren't much different. Kids grow up to become adults and their habits go with them. In some family homes, yelling and swearing is a way of life whereas in others, even a suggestion of disrespect is shattering.

Taking all this into consideration – that there are essentially ten negative comments to every positive one, if you are the person who gives the positive comments, then you are pretty important to your environment.

If you make people feel good about who they are, they will always want to be your friend and ally! They will protect you because you make them feel great. You are an important friend.

Some years ago, a bunch of my closest friends were chatting at a party. Unfortunately an argument started between two girls. One of them was capable of being quite nasty and made horrible comments about me while I was out of the room. Apparently, the whole room suddenly went silent and the girl realised what she had said. No one stood up for me; they didn't need to. Everyone knew that I didn't throw stones, that I couldn't possibly have said the sort of things she was suggesting I did. They knew that she was making it up to help her argument. They knew she was lying. With the sudden silence in the room she quickly corrected her words.

I am not trying to be a hero here, but the incident is an example of human nature. It protects the hand that feeds it. On top of this, I really try to treat my friends well. I write my friends letters telling them how important they are to me and I speak highly of them when they are not around. As a matter of fact, we all treat each other well. We are important friends to each other. They couldn't afford to lose me just as I couldn't afford to lose them. We make each other feel better than anyone else does.

People sometimes go wrong with this strategy because they don't value it. They think, 'Oh yeah, that's nice, next.' On top of that, no one thinks they are guilty of throwing stones, but they are. Let me show you.

At work

Do you wash your cup once it's empty? Leave the photocopier out of paper or jammed? Do you let the phone ring out for someone else to get? Do you hold onto paperwork knowing that it will cause headaches for another department? If you're doing the lunch run do you 'accidently forget' about the person who has made a special request for something? Do you arrive late when you know they need you? Call a sick-day when you don't want to deal with the workload, thus passing it on to someone else? Turn a blind eye to something which is going to cause problems six months from now? Do you leave one sheet of toilet paper on the roll?

If you answer 'yes', you can't seriously value your friends or the people around you. It doesn't matter if everyone else does it. Rise above this. Start a new trend.

What about your partner?

Do you leave the dishes for your spouse, apologising only to do it again ... and again? Do you know that they would love to watch the news but turn a blind eye and watch your show instead? Do you know that they would appreciate a call from you in the middle of the day? A random bunch of flowers? Do you come home late to avoid a task or conversation? Leave the fuel tank empty? Talk them out of things they want to do because you want it your way? Do you insist on sitting in your chair instead of dancing? Insist on going to the footy instead of a theatre show? Spend money recklessly instead of on something important to them? Do you express anger or hatred when you talk about their family?

How can they feel valued? Loved?

At school

Do you borrow money from friends but never return it? Do you borrow paper? Copy homework? Ignore a friend when they aren't invited to a function or when you want to hang out with a 'cooler' bunch of people? Do you find you only hang out with them in the summer because they have a pool? Do you borrow clothes never to return them? Are you rude to your friends' parents? Do you walk on their furniture? Put your feet on the table? Not tell them when you spill something? Lie to your teachers? Exaggerate the truth when you are relaying gossip?

Hold a grudge? Exclude people? Are you sometimes mean? When you know your humour has upset your friend, do you stop?

What about your kids?

Do you look after your body so you have energy for them? Do you tell them to stop being silly? Blame them for your mistakes? Swear at them? Do you trust them? When you say 'no' do you have a good reason or are you just being lazy? Do you blame your tiredness on your kids? Do you think the best days of your life are behind you? Do you speak poorly of your partner? Do you hug them?

How do they know you love them?

This is what I mean about being an important friend. Sometimes we are throwing stones and don't even realise it.

You didn't expect this book to get deep did you?

These rules are significant. Once you learn them, you will be set for life. It will mean that bullies will always feel short around you, and want to pull you down. But you will always be supported and the bully will remain short.

Okay, let's move on to what you really want to know: how to stop a bully.

12 Strategy 5

All the strategies in this book are incredibly effective when used at the right time. This one is gold! I call it 'Blocking Their Path' and it works like this.

Whenever we tell someone that we are not happy with what they are saying or doing to us, they usually respond with an excuse or a reason that makes it look like we are whingeing or that it's our fault. This can be very frustrating because we never get to make our point. They spread stories about what we said and make even more fun of us. The trick I use is to say whatever they would say – but say it first.

Say I want to tell a friend or colleague that I am disappointed in him because each time he is with a certain group of people, he makes fun of me and pretends that I am not his friend. If I come straight out and say this, he will probably answer with something like:

'Don't be silly. I treat you great. You treat me worse than I treat
you. You're always mean to me.'

This probably isn't true at all but he says it to avoid admitting
he is wrong and makes it my fault. To stop this happening, I
point out what I know he will say before he says it. Like this:

'Alex, every time we bump into the guys from the football club
you treat me like trash, making fun and pretending you don't
know me. I know you'll just say that I do it to you but it's just too
obvious, you and I both know it's true.'

I have blocked him so he can't use that excuse anymore. But
what happens now? You got it: he has another excuse. Often
something like:

'Well, you're just so embarrassing, you're such a geek
around them.'

(I realise what is said in response will be different for every
situation but the strategy still works.)

I can block him once again, again by coming in first:

'Alex, every time we bump into the guys from the football club
you treat me like trash, making fun and pretending you don't
know me. I know you'll just say that I do it to you worse but we

> both know that's not true. And you may say that I act like a geek
> around them but we are meant to be friends, it's just too obvious
> that you do it. You and I both know it's true.'

I have blocked both possible answers and Alex hasn't said anything yet. Now, this is my opening. He hasn't said a word and two excuses are shut down. This now allows me to make my point uninterrupted.

If I am not sure how to block someone, I work out what I want to say and then write down all Alex's possible responses. Once I have done that, I write the next thing he might say to avoid admitting blame. It's very simple. Let's keep doing it with Alex so you can see it through.

Here is a list of Alex's possible responses:

> Tell me I treat him worse.
>
> Tell me I am a geek and embarrassing.
>
> Laugh at me and call over some friends to laugh with him.
>
> Say I can't take a joke.
>
> Get really mad and say he doesn't want to be my friend.

You will find that the list always stops. People have a couple of tricks they use to defend themselves, but once they are blocked, they run out of responses.

This is what I would say to Alex then.

> 'Alex, every time we bump into the guys from the football club you treat me like trash, making fun and pretending you don't know me. I know you'll just say that I do it to you worse but we both know that's not true. You may say that I act like a geek around them but we are meant to be friends, it's just too obvious that you do it. You and I both know it's true. I wish you would just back off a bit. Laugh if you want to and call the guys over but it won't change the fact that I am right. And yeah, maybe I can't take a joke but there is nothing funny about this. Maybe I'm not worth being friends with so get mad if you want but if you could back off a bit, that would be great.'

And that is how I get to have my say. It's very simple. It takes some practice but the results are amazing.

You'll also notice that I don't tell Alex to stop doing something in particular. I even invite him to call his friends or make a scene. This is because, as the earlier rule says, if I am strong I don't need to protect myself. So when I invite him to do it, I show that I am strong and not bothered by being outnumbered. I simply will not react.

There are two magic ingredients to making this strategy work. One: always have this conversation one-on-one. Never have it when there is a bunch of people around; they will all get involved and the bully can call on them for help. Two: wait until the bully isn't expecting it. Don't have it while you're arguing. Wait until everything is going well and is normal. The conversation will mean more then.

Let's look at another example. Something more difficult.

Say Becky makes up lies about things you have said and cries to her friends about you. She also yells and screams so that everyone sees what's going on and puts the blame on you. She then likes to gossip about you afterwards, so even if she agrees to your face she will try to get you back later when you are not around. To make the situation harder, let's say you want to talk to her about stealing your friends – which you can't prove.

This is how we would do it:

> 'Becky, I know the first thing you'll want to do is yell and attract as much attention as you can when I say this, and do so if you want, but this is really just between you and me. I am not sure what it is that makes you feel like we can't share friends. I don't want to fight over this, I just want us to be friends with everyone.

> Now I know you'll want to run off and say that I'm crying because I don't have any friends or I'm jealous of something. Later on when I'm not around, you will try to get everyone onside and gossip about me. Go ahead but when you do, know that I know you're doing it. I won't fight you, but I'll know who you really are. We both know it's not about anything else. I am simply saying let's all be friends.'

Just say Becky responds with aggression. This would be expected. That is when we use the 'don't argue' rule. For example, Becky says:

> 'As if I would tell everyone and anyway, you're the one that won't share friends! What about you and Tim? You always hang out. You're the one that won't share friends!'

Even if this is not true, don't argue. Your point has been made. She may not agree with you or want to admit it but she knows exactly what you mean. You can finish now, simply end the conversation. The way to do it is with this magic line: 'Well, if you are right, I guess …' And then say whatever you wanted.

For example, 'Well, if you are right, I guess we will all be friends'; 'Well, if you are right, I guess I won't get pushed out of line anymore'; 'Well, if you are right, I guess I won't get bagged next time the footy crowd comes over.' Therefore, they will only be right if it stops happening, and they always want to be right. This is how to use it in the example:

> 'Maybe I have some things to learn too and I'll make more of an effort. As for you gossiping and exaggerating to everyone, well if you are right, I guess we won't compete over friends.'

Becky will probably think you backed down out of weakness. She is wrong. She will end up the fool because you have stopped arguing whereas she is still going on about it.

Most people, however, will get embarrassed and let it go. Guys tend to respond with something like, 'Shut up idiot. You're such a loser' but this strategy still works. No one ever is going to agree with you on the spot and admit to being a jerk. They will always disagree but the words will echo in their head and you will see a change in their behaviour. Sometimes a little, sometimes a lot.

In the workplace this strategy is dynamite. Very often a workplace bully will use their position in a company or their knowledge of operations to bully people. For example, if they are the boss they will put pressure on you, using money and their control of it as their main strength. It's sort of a 'You need work so do as I say' kind of attitude. Those who aren't bosses can use their knowledge in an area as a way of getting one up on you, either by withholding information or not teaching you how to do things properly. The classic example is sending the apprentice out to buy a left-handed screwdriver; it's a use of knowledge to bully the apprentice into looking the fool.

The good thing is, bullies who use these strategies don't usually have many others, which makes them easy to shut down even though they are intimidating.

Let's say you're an apprentice and every day at work, guys spill things on you, knock you while you drink your coffee, make fun of you in front of the secretary and intimidate you with their physical presence. If only one guy is the culprit you need to have a conversation with him but in a male-dominated workplace where everyone is involved, it is possible to confront the group. You have to judge it yourself, but here is what to say:

> 'Steve, every day I come in here it's the same old routine. Someone deliberately gets oil over my clothes, people knock me as I drink my coffee and then to show off, you do your best to make me look stupid in front of Jenny which makes the whole room feel awkward. And then, as soon as I bring up something like this, you guys puff out your chests as if you're going to beat me up which is fine ...'

then you make your point, for example:

> '… it's just that it's kind of boring. So I thought I would let you know that I understand how the place works now.'

I am not saying get yourself beaten up by being cheeky. I am saying that once you bring up the behaviour and it's out in the open, it takes the mystery out of the magic trick and the fun out of the bullying. It also opens a path for you to make your point.

I once had to deal with a very intimidating and manipulative maintenance man. He would hold onto tools so I couldn't finish projects. He would bring up a mistake I made three years ago and would look for me at lunchtime to embarrass me in front of other staff. He was always giving me a hard time but I never bothered to do anything about it; I rose above it. But one lunchtime in a very public place he called out to me and started bringing up mistakes I had made and then invented things to paint me as a fool. Everyone waited to see what I would do, but I remained unfazed. I started walking away but he called me back. He totally had me.

I finally got out of there but I was furious. Five days later I was walking around a building and he came around the other side.

'Tim, thanks for fixing that shower. Oh, and the other day when you decided to make a fool of me at lunch, you put on a good show but I see way through the song and dance. Pick one mistake and exaggerate it until it's not even true anymore; the way you look to your friends for approval while you dismantle a good man in front of his peers. If that's how you build yourself up Tim, that's fine, but you picked the wrong man. And don't give me that crap about "just joking" or get on your high horse about me overreacting. You were a disgrace that day and I do not deserve to be treated like that. Next time we are at lunch, act as you will, but I'll look you in the eye and we will both remember this moment. Thanks again for fixing the shower.'

He was blown away.

'Wait a second …'

'No Tim, this is not a conversation. Got to go.'

This is a very powerful tool. So much so that the man who everyone feared later came and apologised to me for his behaviour. I didn't get mad, I just said thanks, 'cause I don't throw stones.

So, in summary, the strategy is to block their action or words before they get a chance to say them. Then make your point. If they argue or continue their behaviour, don't argue, just wait it out.

Lastly, it is worth mentioning that to defend themselves, bullies often call in their friends or bring up the situation a week later to embarrass you. If they do this, don't deny your words. In fact, come out and repeat what you said for the benefit of everyone. If it is going to come out into the public, it's best to make sure the facts are straight and that you aren't ashamed of what happened. Once again, this shows strength. It may be uncomfortable for a moment, but this tactic will stop the situation getting out of control and people will really respect you. Remember, the point is not to end all bullying – this would be very unlikely – the idea is to control it so it's not pointed at you.

I do realise that bullies are really good at their stuff and that no matter what I write, there are times when the strategy won't work. It probably won't block the Strategic Bully; you need to use all the strategies to stop them. As for the Home Bully, I wouldn't recommend you use it because when you try this on someone who you are supposed to respect, they might think you are being cheeky. For Home and Strategic Bullies, the next strategy is the one you want to use. It's awesome.

13 Strategy 6

The Secret Weapon: The Journal

This is the one thing a bully can never beat: the journal. I know it doesn't sound very exciting and it probably seems nerdy but I'm telling you that this is a winner.

I'll tell you how to go about it in a moment but first I want you to know why it works so well.

If you have been teased or bullied for some time, you will know that when you approach a teacher, boss or parent, they aren't always a whole lot of help. And not because they don't want to be. Primary school teachers especially have so many kids dobbing in others that they can't tell which cases are serious and which are silly little things that will sort themselves out. For bosses, it is just a hassle they could do without. When you ask for help, your request sounds just like all the other problems of the day.

At a secondary school, a teacher doesn't have as many complaints because people like to handle the issue themselves. Those who do come to the teachers are often more serious cases. The bullies involved usually have some pretty clever techniques, which make it hard for even the teacher to stop them. On top of this, teachers are so busy that even though they want to fix the situation, they have so many responsibilities that they can't give it the time it deserves. They tend to do patch-up jobs. Also, they might not know how serious your issue is, how to help or can't get enough time to advise you properly. The journal fixes everything.

> Use a journal to strengthen your case.

At work it is the same story. The boss hears your complaint but their first thought is: 'What do you want me to do about it?'

People often say that telling a teacher or boss doesn't help, it just makes things worse. This might be because they aren't telling the teacher or authority properly.

Let's say a bully does seven mean things to you. Well, you might be able to handle the first six cases. But the seventh one might be your breaking point and prompt you to tell a teacher or boss. When you do, you only tell them about the seventh offence. For example, if the bully punched you or called you a name, when the the authority figure hears this, she tells off the bully for that particular offence. But soon enough, the bully starts at you again, only in a different way. This time they don't punch you because the teacher told them not to; instead they dream up something else to cause you pain. They have escaped punishment for the six things they did earlier, and they still have a bunch of other ways to bully you. The aim of the journal is to get the bully in trouble for being a bully *all the time*, not just for one offence.

This time when you complain to your teacher or boss, you can show them the journal which contains a long list of the bullying that has occurred over a period of time. It is in black and white and no one can tell you to ignore it now that they can read how serious and constant it is. You'll have their attention. It will be clear that the person troubling you is a bully and not just an infrequent pain in the bum. It's an amazingly powerful tool.

Here is how to put the journal together. You can use an exercise book, loose sheets of paper or whatever, it really doesn't matter but the more organised it looks, the more people will respect it. Always keep everything you write. It doesn't matter if it looks messy, still keep it and stick it in your journal. This way people can see that the bullying has been going on over time and that you didn't just write it all down in one night. When you start your journal, it is okay to write about things that happened days, weeks or months ago but once you have done that, stick to recording things as they happen.

What to write

There are nine main areas that need to be noted. You don't have to do all of them but I really recommend you do as many of them as you can. Remember, it is better to write something rather than nothing.

The nine areas are:

1. Date

2. Time bullying happened

3. Where it happened

4. Who the bully or bullies were

5. What they did

6. What you did

7. Who you told

8. Who else saw what happened

9. Injuries

These are the facts that teachers, parents or police will want to know. It's very straightforward, just write down what happened. The more you can write the better. If you just write, 'He lifted up my skirt' it doesn't say much but if you explain:

> 'We were in the middle of the playground and he kept trying to lift up my skirt but I told him not to. Then he did it again and I couldn't stop him. He called all the other boys to look at me and they made fun of me. Even when I cried they kept doing it all of lunchtime. I sat on a chair near the tuckshop so they couldn't lift it up but they kept dragging me off the seat so they could keep doing it.'

or

> 'I was on my way out the door at 7:30 pm. I had got in at 8 am and worked through lunch. I was just leaving when Gary asked if I had finished my report. I told him I hadn't yet, but that I would do it tomorrow as I was exhausted. He started yelling at me, calling me lazy and saying that my incompetence puts pressure on everyone else. I explained that since Sue left I have been doing two people's jobs but would work Saturday if it would help. He started yelling even more, saying that I was trying to suck

overtime out of him. He told me I had a responsibility to stay until it was done otherwise I wouldn't have a job on Monday. Tim was next door when it happened and heard most of the conversation.'

or

'I wanted to go to Dad's house but Mum said I was too sick to go for the weekend. I said I would rest all weekend and that if she was too tired to drive me, I could call Dad or Nanna to pick me up. She sent me to bed at 5:30 pm, saying I was too naughty to go and that Nanna would never pick me up if she knew how bad I was. But I have been really good this week so that I would be allowed to see Dad. So I asked if I could call Dad to apologise for not coming but she said I was too sick and that he wouldn't want to speak to me anyway. I don't feel very sick.'

It's a shame that we have to do this, but it works. The detail makes people realise how serious it is. Never make things up, just write everything that happened so people can get a clear picture in their head. Sometimes it's easier to write it as a story if you are not sure how to do it.

This journal will get you huge results. Upper management has so much more to work with if there is documentation, as do lawyers, principals and police. Action is taken against crime if there are facts and a journal is well-respected in courts because it is recognised documentation. If you are serious about stopping a bully, you need to get onto this strategy immediately.

The final trick is to keep the journal a secret, but you can tell an adult or trusted colleague if you like. Don't bring it to the place you get bullied, just record the incident on a piece of paper at the time and stick it in when you are somewhere safe.

The bully is powerless against a journal. It proves your point and puts your case in the hands of the authorities.

14 | Time to Act

My experience with these strategies – both teaching them and applying them to my own life – has had an amazing impact. I constantly hear stories of long-time issues between friends being resolved and bullies getting shut down once and for all. My favourite story is about a girl who, after six years of not speaking to her father, used the blocking strategy to stop him from making excuses for his poor contribution to the family. Her mum and grandmother were so surprised that they asked her to teach them how she did it. They too had similar success. And a friend of mine who proofread an early draft of this book then told his workmates about the journal strategy and they each began   documenting unpaid overtime. Upper management didn't know that staff were being driven into the ground.

These strategies are in simple language and explained using schoolyard examples, but people of all ages can benefit from these skills. Like fitness, it takes practice so try using these strategies on smaller issues before you tackle the really big ones. The great thing about these tools is that it takes very little practice to get massive results quickly.

Your biggest obstacle will be your patience. I have had students tell me that the strategies haven't worked and they have lost faith in stopping the bully. But when I question them, I see that they haven't followed the advice accurately.

The most common mistake is with the strategy 'Don't React'. People can hold out for a certain amount of time but then right at the end, they let it all get to them and they react. And later tell me it didn't work. I point out that I told them the bullying would get worse for a bit but they needed to hang in there. Yet instead they let themselves get madder and madder until they blew up and gave the bully what they wanted.

You must sit out their annoying games. This may take one day, or it may last a few weeks until they get bored but *wait it out*. This does not mean you can't respond. You can talk to them, suggest they are being boring or seek help but don't give them the reaction they want.

People can also go wrong with the blocking technique. They do really well and block all the lies and excuses but then their bully says one thing they weren't expecting, and they can't block it. Thus they decide that the strategy doesn't work. In actual fact, it's a matter of practising so now you know all their tricks and comebacks.

It is time to give the skills a go. Remember, only a small percentage of the population takes time to learn these skills. You are now in that minority. You'll be able to use these skills throughout your life. Most of all though, I hope for two things. Firstly, that you use this knowledge to do good. These strategies aren't designed for you to be mean to people you don't like, they are designed to stop people who are mean. I want this knowledge to free you from people so you can be amazing, so that you can be happy and then make others happy. Secondly, I want you to begin the process of realising your capabilities. I want you to enjoy being you and realise that no matter who you are, meanness that has been sent your way has been misdirected; you haven't deserved it so go and sort it out so that you can start to find out what you are really capable of – how talented you are, how smart, how attractive, how likeable and how lovable.

> These strategies are designed to stop people who are mean.

Good luck on your adventure. Please email me your success stories via www.dobbo.com.au and be sure to never stop until you get your life back from the bullies around you.